Emma's Journey

EMMA

authorHOUSE®

AuthorHouse™
1663 Liberty Drive
Bloomington, IN 47403
www.authorhouse.com
Phone: 833-262-8899

© 2022 Emma. All rights reserved.

No part of this book may be reproduced, stored in a retrieval system, or transmitted by any means without the written permission of the author.

Published by AuthorHouse 12/30/2022

ISBN: 978-1-6655-7956-8 (sc)
ISBN: 978-1-6655-7954-4 (hc)
ISBN: 978-1-6655-7955-1 (e)

Print information available on the last page.

Any people depicted in stock imagery provided by Getty Images are models, and such images are being used for illustrative purposes only.
Certain stock imagery © Getty Images.

This book is printed on acid-free paper.

Because of the dynamic nature of the Internet, any web addresses or links contained in this book may have changed since publication and may no longer be valid. The views expressed in this work are solely those of the author and do not necessarily reflect the views of the publisher, and the publisher hereby disclaims any responsibility for them.

Contents

Chapter 1 Departure to the USA 1
Chapter 2 Undercover Identity 3
Chapter 3 People 5
Chapter 4 Sightseeing 7
Chapter 5 The other side of the family 9
Chapter 6 My Child Visited 13
Chapter 7 Joe the weed wacker 17
Chapter 8 Ucare emergency 19
Chapter 9 Runaway 23
Chapter 10 A Strange Man 27
Chapter 11 Reality 35
Chapter 12 Pregnant 43
Chapter 13 High Heel 53
Chapter 14 The City 69
Chapter 15 The Closurer 73

Chapter 1

DEPARTURE TO THE USA

The rain began to fall the entire place looks foggy, the lighting strike everyone was frightened, to my surprised a utility pole was on fire, the rain lashing so heavily I couldn't see anything. I love to listen to the thunder rolling. It sounds like a lion roaring, oh gosh' my siblings are so afraid that they usually run and hide underneath the bed. Steering out of my window I got a tiny glimpse of all the events that were taking place, the trees rocking. wind blowing, in the air it seemed like a freak storm just hit us, finally after a few minutes, theirs was silent, no more lightning struck and the flame died down only smoke remained. I was so impressed to see such bright sunlight, orange colors. What a beauty it was once more. Wow, I keep on thinking about how wonderful the sound of thunder is, a memory that will linger in my mind for a long time reflecting on the great lighting strike, one so powerful with gigantics hits.

Getting ready for work, I get my clothes out, take my shower check to see if my file jacket is in the folder. Comb and groom hair ensure that I get my car key close by then dress. Today I am wearing blue, that's my favorite color. I made a snack pack lunch box, shut the door behind me then drove myself to Deleon House. As soon as I arrived I could hear the dogs barking, they knew that we would be spending my 4 hours here, Nixon was fluffy, and Brooke a little cute blonde sweetest thing ever I have everseen.

My aunt's house has been an important place for me, mainly because it's the house where I always spend my summer holiday and enjoy the majority of childhood memories. A very quaint 4 bedroom house with a big backyard which was ideal for running around and playing hide and seek or jump rope with my cousins and other children in the neighboring community, as well as riding my 2 wheel skateboard. The backyard was accompanied by a semi detached area where my aunt's husband did Carpentry before he died. This area has since become a storage and a laundry.

Chapter 2

UNDERCOVER IDENTITY

The Kitchen was the place where everyone came together and enjoyed a delicious meal. Chocolate cookies were freshly made with iced cold lemonade. The holiday was always special no matter what the season was. Those days I could not wait for school to break, because my family was looking forward to spending this time together. One of the most beautiful women that I have ever known is my aunt. She was a character, very industrious. I will remember her always. Wow I quickly snapped out of my memories and rang the doorbell there came the two dogs rushing toward me. It was Nagi that let me in, she told me of her experience with the current weather. She was more afraid than I think we talked for little, then went on to do my daily duty. Brooke and Nixon has to be groomed before I feed them they love a clean cot, so today we will do catch ball event after play time it's time for storytelling they love to sits quietly with their paws pointing in my directions, sometimes Nixon will roll over and let his ears point up to ceiling making a face to let me know that he enjoying the story. Brooke tries to tap him to get his attention, but he stays

Emma

focused just like a child. Noon it's lunch time. I served them Mochi, Peaches and a bowl of water. Every day after Lunch is nap time because my aunts have scheduled time for them since they were babies, it's their usual routine. A strange phone call, a number which I didn't recognize, was an overseas call. I was a bit nervous. I sit there watching the phone ring for a while, it take around a minutes before i reply hello, hello, it hung up, back then the internet was very bad in Jamaica those days it seemed like the caller on the other end of the line couldn't hear me, so I tiptoed inside the bathroom so that when I returned the call it wouldn't wake up Nixon and Brooke. phone ringing this time the line was clear as crystal. It was a woman's voice, she introduced herself then explained the reason for her calling me. I was astonished. I asked myself why but god knows that my salary was not much so he's providing me the opportunity to migrate to the United States of America.

Chapter 3

PEOPLE

I took the offer and couldn't wait to go home and share the good news with my sibling and my mom and dad. She said that 3 days ago she was going through her diary and found a number of an old friend named Jean so she called her and that's how she told her about her situation and Jean left my number on her voice mail. Nagi went to school no one was there except me, Nixon and Brooke. Nap time up, smiles, smiles my heart was happy with excitement flowing in my veins. The two dogs was ready to go for a walk I share my story with them they too was happy, tail wagging, face light up this tells me that even the dogs are excited we went back play catch with a big brown ball in the backyard, its was almost time to go home, aunt is home from where we stand horn was honking the smell of smoke coming from the car engine. All three of us ran to greet her, Nixon and Brooke were very delighted to welcome their mom home. When aunt opens the front door they rush straight inside dancing, rolling and jumping up and down. My aunt was very petite, weighing about 135 pounds beautiful as an angel. Straight nose and tall fingers resemble her brother who

Emma

is my father. It's payday. I told my aunt about the surprising call that I got today. We sat on the sofa and she encouraged me to take the opportunity and highlight to me about coming to America. She gave me a little change of salary because I would need money for my trip abroad. On my way home feeling generous and elated my mind began to reflect on the outer world. Just my imagination kid in me going to America just watching Law & Order which was definitely my favorite tv show. The busy street, high rising building traffic backing can really handle the fast life. In the 8 minutes I was home I hurried upstairs nervously opening the door. It seemed like my brother heard shuffling the key and the door popped open. Ian was standing there. I grabbed his hand and shouted out Carl, Annmarie and Tameka. We all gather around a tiny dining table in the dining room, Mom and dad hear me and come out of their bedroom. Mom, Dad, I got something to tell everyone. I shared my story to them about the mysterious phone call so my Dad suggested that I tell my Children and also explain how my aunt is saving up some money out of salary to give to me when I am leaving. The children was sleeping so i ate my dinner, mom make pumpkin soup with chicken foot, pigstail, some good old coco, yellow yam, Irish potato, turnip, carrots, rich yellow pumpkin that gave the soup it rich bright yellow color escallion french and grace pumpkin noodle and maggi sup it up. This is exactly what I wanted before taking my shower and off to bed.

Chapter 4

SIGHTSEEING

A week has passed and my children already know that it's almost time for me to get ready to leave summer as past schools reopened in September. I went to work constantly until the first 2 weeks in October. My aunt gave me the money and I hugged and kissed Nixon, Brooke, and Nagi goodbye. I promise that I will always keep in touch and always pray with me, she was a prayer warrior. October 17, 2018. I leave my native land Jamaica. I was a resident of the lust green community Belle Castle in the Parish of Portland. It was very eco friendly, quite cool with great tourist attractions mostly reserved and secured. It's an amazing place to live. lots of coconuts tree bananas, ackees. Portland famous for its rich culture, we are situated on the Eastern side of Island close to Morant Point border between St Mary and St Thomas its the rural area of Jamaica. We lived about 15 minutes from the famous Boston Jerk center known for the best jerk pork, roast breadfruit and Errol Flynn Estate, Blue Lagoon. Reich Fall has a lovely and beautiful Waterfall in the hills surrounded by some giant trees that I have ever seen. Pretty blue spring water rushing from the great Drank Crow Mountains, you can hear the birds chattering in the inhabitants its environment help everyone to relax when anyone from the city visit our beautiful Parish their minds taken away from the hustling and bustling, the sounds of sirens, loud explosion of bullets and cried for help people are free from its pollutants coming from these huge factories that clogged the human minds and blocking their air way from breathing. The freshness of our environment leads these people from all walks of life to enjoy My Wonderful Parish. My journey started with one of the hardest decision that I had made been a mother of five children and four grandchildren living in this rural community where my first marriage crash at the time when things started to Escalade broken down by the shadow threats, rape, mistrust and disloyalty Even After. I was separated from the shadow I once loved called my own. I was repeatedly told by him that anywhere he saw me he was going to kill me. so coming to America will give me peace of mind to heal even though otherwise the children Nixon and Brooke were my real friends. My energy began to fail wondering what, when, where and how to jet away so that I could make a new start at my age. Now I was scared to start life over again. The children had grown up so fast my smile saw us leaving me miserable, my humor getting the best of me. Its drive sparkles fear inside of me all this time. The shadow was a man full of anger, hatred, jealousy. It has become a human disease that he has developed. I call it mental wickedness after joining the Jamaica Constabulary Force back in AUgust 2006.

Chapter 5

THE OTHER SIDE OF THE FAMILY

I never decided to leave my lovely Island so much fun that I used to had in the Sun. I sit and say to myself probably the time is catching up on me, I have to make a change save myself from dying, I left my job in Kingston Jamaica in a quiet community call Deleon where I used to take care of my own student log Nixon and Brooke I enjoyed working with them I was assigned by a company with my aunt I fly to the USA become doubly During On my departure Leaving my children my mom dad behind. My entire family, neighbors and Friends start a new life all over again in a strange place With No tides or assets to my name. Never knew that this day would come after all these years since I last visited London in 1999. That was the best summer because me and all my siblings went to see our other uncles, aunts and cousins. I was spoiled by my relatives because I was the last child for my parents. My second sightseeing was the great Buckingham Palace and a tour on the lovely River Thame. one of the most outstanding exposure that i can remember in my life ever when i was employee for Royal Caribbean Cruise Line i got injury on board their i was deployed to Jamaica departing Vancouver to salt lakes city was so beautiful clean always humid i was delighted to enjoy a fantastic evening at the most attractive ballroom in Canada. Gosh my color is blue so i choose it because it also represent peace life wasn't bad with after all i get to see almost the entire Europe and sailing the Atlantic ocean, Panama canal very adventurous such an amazing historical surrounding the great men from Jamaica, Ghana, Liberia, Nigeria and other who die of yellow fever building this great Canal these were days when I could remember i sit on the plane reminiscing back then I landed at Fort Lauderdale International Airport at approximately 10.30am. I was picked up by a complete stranger. I just spoke with 4 a few times on my phone. I was greeted by the stall and some light-skinned man wearing a pair of glasses. His eyesight was around 5 ft agency's very slim build. I was excited to meet him and he said how was your flight? I said great. I put my small pulley in the trunk of the car then we drove away from the airport, my eyes capturing the scenery Reading Road signs and enjoying the smooth ride. Truly I can say that it wasn't as bumpy as my Rural Road back home in Jamaica. He share much it took us 1 hour and 35 minutes arrive at our destination one I will not disclose it was a big house painted it pink and white with yellow skirting at the bottom and around the edge of the fence I could not help but to notice a camera at the main front door wow I said to myself that this must be a security monitor as I get my foot inside he quickly introduced me to this girl Nikki and tell her to fix lunch for me, then told me that she will instruct me on what to do. He hastily went away, not knowing if my part will be challenging, difficult or amusing. I know for sure that i am not returning to

Jamaica any time soon. I contacted everyone back home to let them know that I had landed safely. Nlkl left me for New York within 3 days of my arrival. She took my number so that we could communicate via WhatsApp. I now have the similar role to play as her. I spend my days cooking, washing, cleaning and ironing for about 5 people this way. My last hope was that the stranger would come in at night to ensure that everything was fine, at times I would cry missing my children dearly as time passed by. I have been here almost 3 months. I shop around for a Lawyer online I got one close by he told me to make an appointment to meet with him so that we can review my document and statement along with police report that I take with me from Jamaica after that I apply to Uscis Immigration for Asylum base upon the threats that the shadow threatened to kill me. I lived at a Disclose address Quiet and peaceful area one that remain Secret won't mention but this place is quite intriguing in Port Saint Lucie the size that I do generate and earning every two weeks it's my only source of getting a little money to survive echoing, voices, trauma, sleepless nights, can't eat twisting, tasking I become very Restless. I was sent to counseling by my immigration lawyer for therapy, my coach was, a beautiful Spanish lady I was given home breathing techniques to help me to sleep at nights, by going every other Tuesday and having my discussion I realize more and more the true sense of not holding on to the past this will help me to let go of my fear. I was once raped, abused, humiliate, threatened by the shadow I once loved and known for several years, going to this place I was healing me slowly, I was even feeling safe been here in the America.

Chapter 6

MY CHILD VISITED

I would freak out at times flashbacks attacking me. I would call the only relative that I could keep contact with is my cousin Rosetta and her two children. Trecia was 4 feet tall, long hair in her back about 8 inches sweeping behind her, straight nose, pale pink lips, and arched eyebrows. She looks like one of the finest models on the stage in Parish. Bud was super handsome. He was wearing a blue jumper outfit with special braces around him. They were so beautiful being Indian and Italian born so you can just imagine the looks of these children. I break away and spend three weeks escaping the trauma of mental breakdown. Coming to America I needed an address for immigration purposes so aunt contacted her and that is the address I gave to immigration to get here. whoever I never bless eyes on them until December 18, 2018. She would take us to the beach a few evenings after she finished working to watch the sunset. Apparently things weren't too great with her either going through a divorce proceeding, but you couldn't tell if she was hurting or unhappy, she was always smiling. We headed back to the house where I was staying. As

Emma

soon as I arrived everyone was so excited. Johnny, Peggy Lee and Hopelene sitting there smiling, putting my bag down on the living room floor walking by quickly with my cousin to the front door we hugged each other then bid bye. At this point I know that I am back to my usual routine. it's almost Christmas there was a note place on the kitchen counter it read your mom call and said that your baby girl will come for the festive season, I was so delighted within a two days she was here she look refined, slim with a lot of hair of hair my parents did a fabulous job she was well taken care of I called Didi, she was excited been her with me, we string the Christmas tree together, hugged each other and pray every day to god to bless us. She helped me to wash the dishes, mopped the floor and folded the clothes. She was worth more than gold, we had an amazing time together during the Christmas season once again i am left alone she returned to Jamaica in January 2019. Her present here was great. It felt like an angel appeared from heaven. It was the happiest 3 weeks of my life. She looks splendid in her blue jeans, lovely, white top. I checked her in at Fort Lauderdale International Airport and waited for her to take off. I encourage her to continue to do well in school and always remember that mommy loves you dearly. Sadly heading back to isolation, a new year still no word from immigration trying to stay in touch with my loved ones back home, everyone was well even Nikon and Brooke, while here at the house I met Leeanna she would come in the days to do paperwork we become good friends because I was in hiding, didn't have a car for myself to go shopping sometimes I would walk to a nearby Mall and be out for about an hour or so, the pianist would come every other Sunday and I sing my favorite song (Great is my Faithfulness) this will inspired me to hold on to my true faith in god as soon as the guy closed the door behind him, I felt alone and empty cold, humid it was winter season still on going, no warm clothing or jacket freezing so bad at night i was given a small heater still wasn't warm very cold I never imagine somewhere would be so isolated, unfriendly and devastating if it wasn't for prayers and faith in Jesus I would have lost my mind completely there are moment when wish I was home with my family who love me unconditionally normally those nights, I cried myself to sleep. laying down just looking up in the ceiling not knowing what else to than to reflect on my own country this was a mysterious journey without answer I myself couldn't understand the chemistry that surround me, o life such a challenge for me been very patient and humble waiting for the right time for god to bless me and take me out of this unbearable situation.

Chapter 7

JOE THE WEED WACKER

My small space for living was a little garage with barely any heat shivering at nights, my thought about life was truly optimistic. Joe used to wacker the yard at times I would say hello to him, marvelously steering at the way he uses the weed wacker cutting the high grass. One day there was a yard sale right across from where the yard was, 1 Was rushing Outside to get me some clothes. The lady's name was Marly and in my hand was only $5 .00. I bought two blouses, and in a short time my money was gone. This peculiar day another lady came by the house. Her name was Fren. She dropped off pastries, milk, meat and fruit. She was a friend of the owner of the house, no one knew my real name, everyone called me Miss Emma. I accept my new identity: it was to keep me safe while at this house. The fact is that I would have to remain hidden in the U.S.A until immigration contacted my lawyer. On the decision they made to know if I was approved to remain in the country, things started to get harder. The job is becoming more intense for me. I have become a modern-day slave no rest at night working 24 hours around the clock. My Tuesday was taken away

Emma

from me. I couldn't argue because I had no other dwelling. No, I'm sucking salt to the Wooden Spoon I've kept in my mouth. On Friday I bought an LG phone to keep in touch with a past associate in Jamaica just to stay focused and positive. This will keep my mind active surprisingly i feel a sharp and sudden pain in the of my head so terrible seem like electricity running up and so much pain leaving me devastated omg so frightened Lisa took my vitals sign and it was blood pressure that knock me down by this i call the undercover man to take me to see a Doctor having only $50 remaining in my name this will be a challenge for me. My medication is completely finished and there is no more supply in store. He didn't arrive until 40 minutes later.

Chapter 8

UCARE EMERGENCY

When we arrived at the emergency room on SE Port St Lucie Boulevard, he was in a rush. He dropped me off and left. I hurried up to the information desk to get some help. My first question I asked was if the services were free here? The receptionist said no I was shocked she then asked me if i have Health Insurance my answer was no for the second time around she then told me that i need to pay $89 to see the Doctor, I felt so embarrassed in a nice way i said thank you and leave the building walking and thinking, talking to myself still having tingling on and off pain all over my face, neck, and my head. My mind flashes by on the lady who supplies the food for the house. I remember taking her number. I quickly searched my phone contacts until her name came up. I called her with no response, then tried to reach the mysterious stranger who dropped me off. He was not available either. My only hope now was Fren. I rang back once more eventually she answered, explaining the situation and giving her my location. She didn't hesitate to come and take me to an Emergency Room on Darwin Square. My mind flashes back to my Doctor in Jamaica so drained and lost I was quickly seen by the health team without delay Thank god I become scared and frightened my mind was on the children I asked myself this question I might going to die leave them behind especially Sunni still pulsing in my mind but while I was there I keep on praying for god to save me I thought for a moment that my journey mysteriously come to an end But oh I fight' on with winter coming to a closure I apply myself to my living situation and come to know I have to trod on by faith. when I returned to the undisclosed destination I told the man that I'll be leaving with Miss Fren taking my suitcase so that I park pieces of pia, pia, because I sent back the small pulley to Jamaica with my daughter Unable to get a date, day, or time to when this man will give me the go-ahead to Venture in a New Direction. One morning I run away with Miss Fren being transfer from one place to the next I was impressed another beautiful scenery big yard space I was greeted by this huge female dog name Nana, Oh my God she sprang right up in my arms fran to get her to settle down, at the house it was persons Chris, Thersee, Pat and Coreen a retired nurse and an ex-soldier I meet her in December 2018. Coreen wasn't any stranger to me; she was at the same place with me where I was isolated and locked away from the world. She greeted me with a hug and a big smile. In the living room was a lemon green 3 piece sofa set, 48 inch television hanging on the wall across the hall were a small brown coffee table, there was a little room containing just a single bed, a Black and white printer a longline telephone, Cabinet stock with files and medicine locker, there was an open space close by the entrance of the room with nothing to stop other people from seeing me undress. Nana was giving a few behavioral talks with Fran telling her that it is safe to be around me and giving reassuring words. Nana put up her right foot into Fran's hand before she left to show that she understood what was said. Lunch time I washed my hands and prepared a warm meal and served a cold sandwich for everyone. Cris was like the Chief in command, he took care of the dog even the rest of residents who resided in the house that very they had a visitor it was case manager, fact team and a guidance counselor to engage socially and interact with these in house residents. Fran came by at 6.45pm to pass medication after supper before all 4 persons went to bed. It was 3 weeks now that an at my new location I call my siblings, children and parents and tell them about my escape from this wicked and cruel man my dad was very worry for but I caution him not to worry but continue to pray for me mom was delighted to hear my voice, and for my siblings they wanted to know more about America everyone was excited we talk for hours I was at Fern Circle nothing much to attract me still hard work less stress a wonderful family Flora who is fran sister in law sometimes stop by for a day or two giving me time for myself feeling comfortable been able to sleep now was a sign of relieved I am now familiarized with each and everyone on weekend it games night Thursday movie nights Tuesday we chill outside in the backyard playing soccer, some smoking, laughing and having fun. Nana am i get along well I love dogs from back home she was nothing compared to Nixon or Brooke she was weighing around 75 pounds gray in color, big paws, strong legs firm body muscular like shes is lighting weight bright green eyes whenever we are outside she would be in a fenced area with her a bowl she was happy to be around us. In

February, I contacted my lawyer and changed my mailing address to this new upscale dwelling so peaceful time flew fast. I received a letter from immigration I was approved to stay in the country with a fixed date to go in for biometric. The kind hearted lady drove me to West Palm and i did my fingerprint she took me back home few weeks pass actually a month i received a call from the law firm they have got my results back from uscis office there was any interview date set for me as yet but i was comfortable with the outcome god is good all the time. Nana love to take her bath on Friday. O my, she loves the water splashing swimming around and playing with her toys she was very smart and communicate well i began to enjoy everything around her no stress thank god for his grace i pray in season and out of season life change so much and i was afraid again because my environment was friendly not boring and with Nana been here it was amazing, amusing, and excited.

Chapter 9

RUNAWAY

Exploring the new era of life, a new Community which is full of Historical, Botanical Garden, Shopping Centre Beauty salon and various Diners. Cris usually goes out on Fridays but I never ever seen his companion. I know that it was a man but he never entered the building, he would call before coming. I sometimes answer the phone or There would as well. on this Friday the doorbell ring so I open the door their stand a well groomed black man very handsome muscular around 5feet 7inches tall the smell of his cologne was so refreshing bowed leg well dream her said am here to pick up Cris very soft tone i let him know that he will be right there within a few minutes closing the door behind me wow my heart beating fast blushing away smiling to myself I never meet anyone like him since I been here o lord, anyway outside in the backyard was nice and sunny whenever it's like that i occupied myself in the garden cleaning and transplanting all the beautiful flowers this keep my mind stable and not worrying much about anything. Months had passed since I heard from my cousin here who resided close by. When I am lonely I could call Niki in New

York so that we could chit chat about life back home and our youth days growing up in Jamaica. Cris when again, now surprisingly he told me that Frank likes you smiling away then I asked him who is Frank? He jokingly replied to my companion, he laughed and walked straight to his room. We never had another discussion about the subject again for a long while. Miss Fren made sure that everything was fine at the house she worshiped on the Sabbath so on a Saturday whenever she is not around i will have to do extra things around the house basically it wasn't anything hard light duties. Coreen and I would take long walks and talk about her life and her brother David whom she love very much her career expanded from a Nurse to an Army veteran she was beautiful she very dangerous due to her illness but I love her she at refused her medication this is when she wants to fight with me or the rest off the residents she love rootbeer her speciality Thresse would go by the Gas Station and ensure she bring back one cold rootbeer for Coreen she was treated exceptionally well My children would WhatsApp me to check up on me and ensure am doing find Sunday was our contact day what am amazing family. Dad got sick. He was diagnosed with Manic Dementia and depression. Now my mom is Diabetic also been here. I have to check up on whether their health hasn't gotten any better or any worse. I pray to god everyday for hours to bless me because I know that I am not returning to Jamaica. This Sunday my call was earlier than usual. I could hear crying in the background. My sister Buzie told me about our dad being hospitalized due to poor health. He was unstable and unable to do anything for himself or communicate with anyone. It was very hard that Miss Fren had to rush me to Darwin Emergency Room. High Blood pressure hit me cold. I was given medication and was back home again. I started to keep track of my father daily until he was discharged from the hospital.

Chapter 10

A STRANGE MAN

Then this handsome man came back this time he was bold that ask me for my number I gave it to him, and hurry back inside feeling sexy and appreciative I told my family and my cousin who worked and lives in New York that I met someone they were happy for me knowing that I have been single for more than 5 years with me being separated and also, divorce and I never intended to be engaged emotionally. I open up my heart to love again. Being battered and scarred deeply With all the dramas that hit me like a tornado, dating was the last thing on my mind. Hey I'm not going The weekend past then i received a text from the saying hi I text back saying good morning Frank he told me that he's at work now ok then we talk soon on march 15, 2019. One day he asked me out to dinner. I told him that I am not sure about it because within myself I was afraid of trusting any man again. Just healing from my past and protecting me is very important. Toni is my confident she lives in London and my cousin Mia who is super loyal she is a Teacher in Jamaica I tell them about this handsome dude they were not doubting it but warned to look out for sign and to be observant a lot he continue to asked me out once more i refused and was hesitant we went to dinner, He arrived at the house 1.45pm after he leave work pick me up and we drive he smell like fresh wild berries, is teeth white and shiny clothes neatly iron he was wearing a green shirt with a sheen of green, with silver pattern a ring on his finger, clean shaved, shine black shoes seams in the front of his blue jean straight like bow & arrow I was surprised that we actually match Frank appearance drew me wild their and then i become attracted to him has a human being my emotions was boiling i was steaming hot, we went to a Buffet his favorite restaurant I haven't been out for more than 5 months since in the usa enjoy the evening out it was great. we left the restaurant on our way back home he got a call then we headed t6hat to his apartment welcome to Leacock Run I observed every where my eyes lightening up to see the lovely scenery of this place he step out of the vehicle come around and open my door for me has any gentleman would we walk upstairs he lived on the second it was so cold inside he had the thermostat on 65 degree he asked me if i was cold so i told him yes he then lower the temperature turn the air condition down to 70 degree but quest what is apartment was clean just like him 2 bedrooms, 2 bathrooms he introduce me to his roommate Frank when to use the bathroom then he whisper Emma I like you very much, I pull away, time was against us, it was almost dark black thick clouds it might rain. When I returned home Fran was expecting me back by 5pm. He held me by my hand and we walked out the door together on our way back. He was quiet for a minute. It takes us a short time to arrive at my destination. We bid me goodbye then left. Life change for me now I found a friend after that Sunday every weekend we go out to dinner after work he stop by to ensure we spend time together getting to know each other, months pass and he asked me if i would come and live with him because he didn't like my living situation my eyes start to see strange place I felt like someone care for me therefore I take the offered Fran give me the go head but she wasn't please with the deal Frantz got for her he decided to dropped me off to work in the morning so then i will be at home in the night o dam she get mad it won't if she leave she leave for good so we leave one friday evening i keep in touch always when I have anything important to do I still call she become my mom here very supportive until this day.

    Romance, sex, fun, love, we got it all his soft voice, his gigantic body, thick i get so accustomed to rub my my hands all over his body he would get horny so get especially when I massague his body gentley using vitamin E oil to seduced him, watching his hot, sexy and shining body was so attractive been muscular is back was arched so deep and firmed so gorgeous the love was getting stronger everyday he was an Aquarius and, I am a Sagittarius we craved for sex. Sometimes we would take pictures and enjoy our own company. When he held me and kissed me I would breathe so hard and wet myself full of an organism so in love with Frank. He been asleep and I would use my tongue to tickle is entire body from neck straight down to his spine he would turn over and make passionate love with each other he was so sexy we usually take hot steaming shower continuing to stimulate each other we would mourn and groaned is desperation hungry and thirsty to feel the sensation rising between my legs he beg me to tightly he

Emma

was shaking vigorously, Frank beg me Emma to make love to him knowing this he was a smoother we would enjoy pleasuring each other gracefully we shuffle out the bathroom kissing, hugging, water dripping he lower me in bed he was so strong imagine been pick up like a feather he position me carefully and pour honey over me this was toxic to our soul. He therefore place me in any position that pleases him, he is an Haitian, he would speak in his own native language which is creole, gentle whispering my ears breathless saying bang (zuzu, zuzu) cohen doz zuzu with me wetting more and sweating heavily I lay him on his back and ride the way he touch my body, let my heart beat so hard, I can't control my ego for him. Frank become more advanced in the bedroom our relationship was sparkling, life remain great no problems just love and emotional june 2019 he had to renew his daughter passport we were going through some papers when i found out that he was married shock I was lost for words couldn't believe this life is full of surprises and the he was quite cunning I now know that he wouldn't make me a wife, suddenly within a spilt minute my face changed, dramatically the mood of the love clogged the atmosphere of love become sour our relationship continue in spite of the true which open my eyes more sometimes i would question him saying when are you going to divorce this woman. Frank failed to respond and in disbelief it felt like a hurricane hit me. I was embarrassed by the fact that he had lied to me to get me where we wanted, a very contradictory soul held in captivity over shadow, blind, deceived, rustling, against this demonics attack that plagues my mind. He had conquer me into falling for him in a discrete way i was a fool to love, sometimes i get angry but i didn't express it very disturbing, fear Frank secret come out even himself was astonished. One week after things settled down we lived at the same place no changes school will be out in Jamaica and he agreed for my children to come and visit us for the holiday. Being around him I have no choice other than to stay with him while the children are here. No one knew about this in the US. My daughter, who has a godmother From Fort Myers, was going to Jamaica, her expected husband, so she will take the children back with her when she returns to the United States of America. Flight was booked and everyone was excited time to travel my mom ensure that they were set and on their way, things went bitter when I received a call from my friend that she just check the children passport and realized that her god daughter will not be making the trip due her jamaican passport expired, I paused for a while then tell her to repeat what was said so astonished in disbelief wanting to hold her so much all i could do was to contact Jetblue and let them placed the money in a travel bank account everything was put in place by the airline. I was lost for words feeling sad, we were already on our way to the airport hitting I - 95, phone ringing it was one of frank friend calling him from Haiti he been occupied talking on the his mobile phone waiting for him to talk with me my thought was very far in shocked, I swallowed so hard, just to hold back my tears. He was off the phone so I explain the situation he console me with words of comfort which builds my confidence, that she will be here with us soon My son call once more we talk i told the taxi driver what that he have to take her back to the country my mom will be at home waiting for her it a difficult moment for me not been able to hold my baby girl oh, she cried, and cried until she fell asleep, time went by quickly and my son was here with us, so excited 2 hours had pass he clear custom and was give 6 months stamp in his passport we greet one another Fiona son pick her up and all three of us drive home so exhausted, tired and drained we settle in nicely show my son to his bedroom i had prepared dinner we eat joke for a while then watch the news up getting my spices and jerk seasoning that my mom send for me nutmeg roast breadfruits, ackee chocolate dry promento and the good old jamaican white Rum. Packaging the things in the kitchen cupboard then exiting the living room straight to bed couldn't stay up any longer because it was a long day, hot, and frustrated o life never easy, always something going on but the day ended just as it was supposed to go. There was so much to be thankful for. I Am glad that my son was here with me. I was smiling again. He was so tall I couldn't believe my eyes were very slim just average size for his age. Miss Rowena who always in her garden planting her plants never dress has a farmer nails well paint big orange straw hat sun shades glass with her shovel and water love to stop Frank and talk for even 2 minutes she wear bright red lipstick

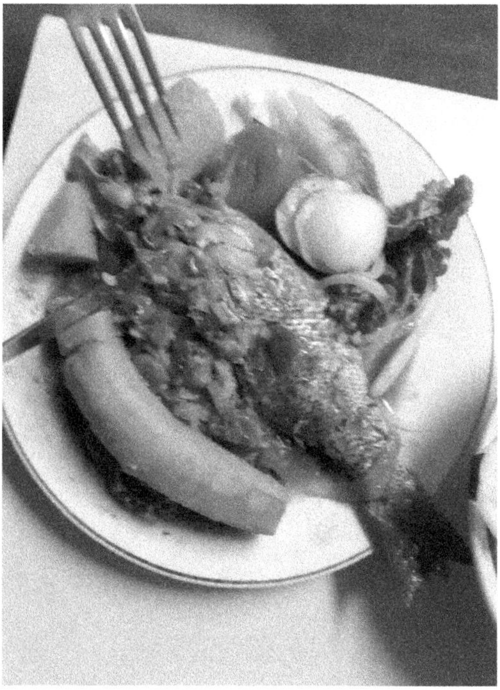

Chapter 11

REALITY

In the morning when we got up, I made breakfast for everyone, while Frank was in the shower Blackberry raspberry, and an egg sandwich one of favorites with lettuce tomato slice, hot lemon tea. It's a new day, a new beginning. We got a lot to talk about me and my son Sunni. This is his second visit to the United States of shower Sunni, still in bed resting from a long flight here oatmeal, strawberry, America. Frank at breakfast and left for the day its was awfully quiet I went on the balcony am I going to see you If the Squirrels were outside running up and down the tree, looking for food to eat it was, 9 am my son was up he didn't want the oatmeal so he fried egg and bread. He told me the great story about unemployment plaguing Jamaican no jobs for the Youth them crime and violence Rising, in the inner city especially Kingston, Clarendon, and Montego Bay, police killing an all kinds of things happening he told me it was getting bad gun for drug trade I said hmmm, that wasn't too surprising for me, life change people change, the world is changing the society losing it touch from reality this is the real it was on the news lately. Phone rang. It was mom on the line. She was happy to know that he arrived safe. Everyone was excited, even the baby girl was happy for him being here. Can you imagine the excitement in the background? I could hardly hear myself so we wished them all the best and enjoyed the summer holiday. Sunni sold his Motorcycle before he left home. I pray constantly for my family and give god thanks that they are all doing fine in the country. Frank would do anything actually to make my son feel at home. He would try to give us a lot of jokes reminding us of his youth days growing up in Haiti. He told us some men never have footwear in those days they would paint their foot with white paint, browns paints, or black paint so that the ladies think that they are wearing shoe but little did these men known that there was trap set in the house for them nails set in pieces of board lying on the floor, so has soon has the man enter the house you could hear screaming then everyone could laugh about it because he was bear footed i laugh, and laugh until I cry Sunni cried too, Frank was so funny delighted by his story every country have it culturally differences, the summer was well spent we had a lot of fun we would go all over the state of Florida on most weekend church it was significantly the weather began to change with summer coming to an end the adventure of sightseeing, so many beautiful scenery and lovely attraction, waterfall, especially Seaworld places that will reflect in my mind for many years after it was awesome. The sunshine city has lots of attractive variety of destinations, large aquarium with unfamiliar sea creatures and mammals oh what a beauty, hundreds of different kind of birds so colorful the Leacock was the most elegant species walking timely across the street they It seemed like they were modeling on the red carpet in Miland so proud with an upright posture it was my first encounter with this beautiful bird. Back to reality summer is over, time is winding down for my son's departure and I still got another week to spend with us. Tuesday morning the man of the house decided that we all drive down with him to fort lauder to check up on his taxes that he had filed. We were there with him for over six hours so I asked him for something to eat and he told me that he didn't have any money. Sunni now telling me that he's so hungry i couldn't come to my senses, an argument develop right there on the spot where we all sitting in the car about this boy been hungry i got no job so no money leaving me penniless my heart bleeding I work hard back home with my aunt taking care of Nixon and Brooke just to provide warm meal daily for my children, my siblings and my parents so never in my life time was anyone of my children cried for hungry this man was vicious, m cold hearted and wicked the scenario happen we drove back home i could barely stand up so i quickly make dinner we eat but my heart was still heavy days went by Sunni left for home he arrived safe my mom was waiting for him at the Airport i send back a few sovereigns from our trip in summer e everyone was grateful no peace in the apartment since then i now started to see a complete different side of this man he get so catch up of doing him and not concentrating on our relationship and constantly arguing or silent treatment now it was about simple things that we would laugh over. He stop buying food in the house I have to call his sister in New Jersey to speak with him everything has changed this man was so serious, vicious and dangerous un comparable to anyone I know he had a food stamp card for his mom that we used to buy grocery with I remember quite vividly asking what is the problem this change between us was strange but real. The relationship becomes sour. We stayed in each other's lane just to keep our sanity and peace in the home. It was very silent, separating from each other. I've become so uncomfortable that it wasn't good to become sad, miserable, unhappy. no one night I asked him when will you submit your divorce paper he stiffen and remain quite not to answer me I said don't ignored me, it's about time you man up and do what you got to do or else I'm leaving this house this very moment, before he could answer me the phone ring it was ex-wife, his child mom she's the only girl that he got he barely speak of her or hold a conversation about his child she told him that he have to come and sign some passport form to get the child passport renew he didn't want to go he so get mad he was upset raging an cussing out the ex wife in a rude way I told him if you love me you will have to go and do this for your child I figure that things was complicated between them, but my concern about what going on with them i care zero the child was my concern. he went on and get it done that too was passed. We continue our journey of love together, our friendships restored November now we drive downtown to the courthouse and get the divorce papers to fill out and returned as soon as possible after talking to an agent he realized that he had to do this to move on with his life I would be his fourth wife the third wife was in Haiti he married to her 2015 wow that was very impressive from this man, he was someone to be loved no matter what happen you know how to smother and Charm a woman very seductive soft spoken his mouth full of spice from the island he was very convincing gentle to touch. In any way that I wasn't able to resist him after the summer ended, life got miserable. I could not hold my tears back. I was missing my son dearly. Sunday around 5 a.m. I was in my deepest sleep and could feel the mystery man inserting inside of me oh my God I was draining for a long time its been over two months i just open up and enjoy the ride so thirsty i miss him we never make for a long while now it was a captivating moment I felt like i was drinking streaming hot, sweating even though the air was cool this man body is super attractive it kills me when we are together, we become compatible with each other we are so much alike when it comes on to the bedroom no jokes about that we were craving for each other no matter the situation we enjoy sex it feel like the first time we meet each so it was great, women love a good jockey one that is full of compassion i see star light flashing we were in another world just like fifty shade of gray we climax together i was relieved comforting we each other every time this happen we saw that it was worth it. Oh i felt like i just had been attack by a hungry tiger, cruel, mean, but quit playful we close that chapter 3 week in November miss Fran call me she said that there is a letter for you from Immigration i couldn't wait for Frantz to get home to tell him the good news the letter was pick up my work permit arrived i skipped, sing and dance i thank god I was the happiest person in the world This is a new beginning for me a turning point in my life that i get my independent back am ready for work it was a blessed moment for me today I'm going to bake a cake, steam fish boil plantain and prepared salad so that we can sit and eat and give glory to god. The evening was kind of chilly than always cool breeze blowing outside So I sit on the balcony call my family but home to tell them that i am out of the mystery in my life a big break for me to send my children the money required for school because I strongly believe in education and want the best for them. Monday morning I went job hunting Frant drop me off at a plaza on Port St Lucie Boulevard up and down the plaza knocking on every business door My first stop was a senior living and memory care unit I fill out an application an move on I make a second stop at Smoothies and cafe shop the sign said we are hiring now I went in and asked for the manager she came out with a wide smile like she just won the jackpot a million dollars we sat down together outside and share my experience with she told me to sit and wait for a while hurriedly this blonde, blue eye lady went back inside from where was I see her talking to another lady when she returned she interview me to my surprised the lady employee me right on the spot she told me to stay working Wednesday morning i was amazed by her offer in my whole life i never get a on the spot job I walk back home it took me 35 minutes to do so Frank was at work so i had no other choice than to put my foot in my hand and hurry on it wasn't hot because it almost December i talk to god on my way i pray constantly l take a shower and jump straight in my bed lord have his mercy the excitement began as soon as my love arrived from work I went to greet him at the door jump up in his arms and tell that got a job he said Emma am happy for you, we make love right there on the floor in the living room we didn't care about anyone more than ourselves, we shut the world out for a brief moment we love to shower together after that its was time for dinner. We ate and went to bed. It is getting colder now winter has arrived, it's just around the corner. There was no washing machine in our apartment. Now I have to go to the laundry. This is very challenging and more intense pulling these big garbage bags across the playground up to the area for washing with me. Starting a new job we barely see each other and I didn't have a ride Sometimes from what's the stock price to drop me off even those things start to get better we open an account together and I apply for the internet starting to contribute to the rent, our roommate move out after all the contrary situation drama he was getting involved too much because they were from the same country, and I didn't like its a compromising position lead mean now to face desperate imagination living there with so many obstacles. Dear December I welcome you this my birth month and father too we are both Sagittarius excitement in the air with Nagi coming from Jamaica am in a good mood. Frantz gave me $100 to put with the money that JetBlue had in the travel bank account for her to be accompanied by an airhostess because she was a minor and was allowed to travel by herself. We become distant from each other now more than ever but my love never change for this man, he started to go out without me places like Miami, Fourtlauder thing take a turn for the worst sometimes he get home 12am in the no call, no text nothing if i call to find out if he was ok no respond we were hardly at home together this was the second week in December my birthday was almost here I asked him if we could go out to dinner on my birthday because it a special day for me to celebrate and enjoy the evening. He had all kind of excuses why he won't be available to go with me it just tension arising from nowhere again this seem serious i thought to myself, hiding everything now from me, eating by himself staching thousands of dollars in his carnot been open and honest anymore every conversation is just lies, lies on top of lies i try not to get upset and play the fool and his game now we never fight physical but i demonstrated my woman strength by exercising my right to let Frank see that he was slipping away like an eel not showing an sign of caring about my emotional well being. I then realized that is past life has destroy him and know he is blinded this man can't accept true love he lost his moral value and now he's haunted by fear, the mind was plague with mental wickedness and no woman could understand this mystery only god can solved his problem I prayed always for new transformation and inner healing he need to be restored. My birthday pass is spent in my room. December 11th Nagi was coming mom call to say that they leave for the airport fine we drive to get her she didn't arrived on time flight got delay in KIngston, Jamaica Jetblue landed she was so excited she run straight in my arms she was very slim we hugged each other for a while mom i miss u, omg heaven rejoice and angels was singing and dancing I was wonderful blessed to have here once more thank god. We decided that she should live here with us we apply to Port Saint Lucie School District and she was accepted an was enrolled as a student at West Gate K-8 school within walking distance from our apartment.

Chapter 12

PREGNANT

On December 20th I found out that i was pregnant am becoming a mom again jollyful feeling right in the middle of the festive season we prayed to god for 10 months to be conceived over excited I run to frank and told him the good news to god be the glory great things he has done. I quickly spread the news to my family, friends and my siblings and the rest of my children wow i was full of hope ready ready for this child to join us I started to shop on Amazon we named the baby. Christmas was like a few days away. We decorated the tree and placed all the gifts under it. we had an amazing holiday Nagi love him dearly she always sit up and waited to hear frank keys rustling the door she would run and hug him. Spring School reopen for Nagi Frank drop her off to school each day and ensure that she was safe after he leave work in the afternoon he pick her up and take her home Nagi and him have a great bond that she began to call him Daddy that so sweet. Oh so Charming. Humble and attentive and I was happy to have her around, Naji has her own room, the same room that Tayler moved out of, our nights are quiet after she completed her homework, we would watch the news before going to bed. She lights up our world and brings a unique change in all our lives. We had was to get her polo sport to wear to school to be a new student in a strange environment for her she tried to fit in very well I this time she met all the children one of the girls would come to the door and knock since we live at that Apartment 203 no one ever come by we were very enthusiastic take to hear the sound of banging at the door magic get familiarized with the children so quickly he did not like it at all we used our Sunday to visit a very popular Catholic Church. Najee and I was a Christian a true baptist believer we were baptized in the Baptist Church in our community in Jamaica, not having any ride for ourselves our only option is to go with Frank it was a peculiar Way for Najee to worship, she would say Mom do I have to kneel down I would whisper softly yes my dear, when they sing she paused and observe the different kind of singing this really just an unknown culture that she has no clue about sometimes magical i guess with smile I would imagine of what she was thinking, I thought of it because I was once in your shoes she seems a bit puzzle, it take her a while to get acquainted with the Catholic Assembly she was kind friendly and loving like to hug me. Sunday is our best day at home I normally prepare or favorite dishes chicken, steamed fish, fresh lettuce and tomato, onion, avocado, boil plantains or bulgur because we did not eat rice our drink would be pineapple with ginger no sugar added so refreshing after dinner then dessert for everyone a slices of watermelon for frank and strawberry pie for us. Our household was always conscious of the way we eat we are healthy eater, vitamin is a must taken by everyone at home only me was sick with chronic illness i was suffering from high blood pressure he tries to stay healthy always before We were together he was told that he got diabetes and you was acting classes for a while then this was control in a few months he didn't reschedule a doctor appointment until October 29th. This time he had been tested by Doctor Boyd. His blood sugar was a bit I the Night before Easter holiday and he ate two packets of cookies containing two dozen in the entire sachet. I asked him are you not going to see your doctor in the morning? he responded Emma I am fine I started to laugh I was cracking up we drink a lot of water throughout the night I would put 3 head of gar out of garlic sand 3 clove in the water at night we would pray before sleeping giving thanks to God for his Blessing I was conceived a baby on the way, we have accomplished what we asked for we repeat the 23rd psalms every single night that was our team in the morning we will do the same for 10 full months at this time we put our order confidence in God believe in the doctrine and the word of God we pray for entire family for them to find Inner Peace front never have a favorite color he loved multiple Shades shapes and various forms of clothes I prepare is clothes work and make breakfast before leaving for my work each morning at 6:35 a.m. Every single morning, life was good. After a few months I resigned my job at Tropical Smoothie and became a full time employee at a Senior Living and Memory Care Unit. Attending orientation i took 13 exams in one day pass all of them i was offered workplace benefit dental and vision none of my children were eligible so i had was to put him has my beneficiary because he was the only one with a social security number whoever everything was in place he has my emergency contact my position was RCS I didn't have my CNA OR HHA certificate all I have with me was a LImited Mental Health certificate am now 10 months pregnant Frantz seem a little bit frustrated and worried i try to reassured him that things will be fine going forward with us and the baby communication now becoming harder mood swing the love is not spicy anymore one day he turned to me and said Emma I can't afford the baby because i got both car insurance to pay car to fix and it hard for me, I sit him down and told him a child is not a challenge i will save $100 from my salary each month and if you save $20 or $50 out of your pay every 2 weeks we can save enough money to go shopping by may. He was very confused About what you wanted to do. Things between us start to change. I'm feeling disappointed, sad, hurt and miserable. I question myself and ask God if he's going to let history repeat itself curiosity was killing me we couldn't let Nadia see the change that I continue to pray one day we drove up to TD Bank on Saint Lucie West we had a brief discussion I recall telling him that if I'm alone she sacrificed and shop for this baby I will take you to court for child support friends told me that he's prepared and he will tell the judge that I got five other children and you will get full custody of the child he was change completely. this was what I was running away from the mistress the lies and deceit The Daily Show is ugly face and said war he feel like I am not noticeable about it I did the drug and alcohol test in November and pass the exam it was time to go to DMV office to get my license told me if I get my license and his ex-girlfriend's image driving the truck she's going to kill me I was lost over then I replied and said kill me for what if you break off a relationship

Emma's Journey

with someone why would this person want to kill Emma I swung become fearful my mind thought soul and body thinking about what direction we are heading towards now we are arguing more than ever friends tell me that you didn't want me for his wife we are only good friends and he's helping me I start to cry and packing my stuff up but I have nowhere to go I still remain in the house I'm the house helper having my eleven-year-old daughter with me in a situation Give me no choice more than to Bear the cross like Jesus, I start to blame myself feeling depressed I'm thinking suicide now I am going back in time or life because my child was in Jamaica she was very comfortable I know he'll Popular MMOs I was totally confused France always said I'm not showing you out it's up to you if you want to leave I was in my first trimester pregnant life seemed very miserable and uncomfortable now I had shoes on my foot I start to you life in different ways I am in a strange place with no family support I couldn't sleep at night I become more vulnerable I become a work I did I couldn't sit down I work non-stop until my shift was ended I use this tragedy that no one noticed any kind of difference going on I was dying inside my director and co- worker didn't know that I was stressed I was so stressed could not imagine what life was going for me I met Jen we become closest of friends I start to share my story house since I got pregnant my relationship is broken down so rapidly and things deteriorating fast like a piece of land eroding. we stopped sleeping together separate from each other he's on the left I'm on the right all by ourselves, sometimes I sit up in the closet thinking how can we fix this problem the man began to get ignorant, ignoring me more and more you would spend hours on his cell

Emma

phone not even notice that I exist anymore wow it it me like rock bottom but I keep on praying never letting go of my faith in God January 25th 2020 I got up to take my shower prepare breakfast and get ready for work when I step inside the bathroom I realize that he hide the toothpaste it was nowhere inside I called him three consecutive time and ask him where is the toothpaste he use Sensodyne brand so he got up fast out of his bed like a madman I was standing in the middle of the bathroom door he shoulder Shoved me so I held onto the front of his shirt and asked him why you hiding a common toothpaste from me? We do not share toothpaste I use Colgate to whitening but I gave it to my daughter because hers was finished the day before you reply you being smart so I asked him again what are you talking about Oh please I said imagine I am here washing, cooking, cleaning, and carrying your child in my stomach and you are here hiding a common toothpaste Lord have mercy she flashed my hands All Phase shirt my hand hit him on his lip and he starts shouting at me then he began tossled with each other he grabbed my left breast so hard ice cream out you're hurting me then he squeezed me in the stomach I tried to get him off me this is when I fell in the shower the curtain tore down I get up quickly got to brush brush my teeth when I get out of the bathroom you were sitting on the sofa in the living room I told him that I'm ready to go to work it happened with a split sweet 5 minute you drive me to this senior living and memory care unt on California boulevard off Port St Lucie West I step out the vehicle and remind them to please remember to pick me up at 3 p.m. this Saturday I called one of his best friend to let him know what happened this was done during my lunch break, I also called his sister Arelene and explain the situation. My shift came to an end, he was right there outside waiting for me. I got home doing my womanly duties as a housekeeper. What has become lately? I made them dinner and nothing happened on that Sunday. It was just silence between us, no tension. on next day approach it was Monday still no communication between both of us we didn't display any form of anger to let Najee see that there's a problem in the home I wake up to take my shower at 6 a.m. as usual after and rested in the bathroom in my underwear there was blood I was shocked frightened and shaking I shout Sam, sam, you got to wake up, wake up, sam I am losing the baby please take me to the emergency room, my heart pounding hard I began to breathe heavily get dressed and rush off with me he was super quiet not talking I stopped at Walgreens get a pregnancy test kit and contact my job to let them know that I can make it in this morning due to an emergency i am going to the emergency room. We arrived at this huge orange and white emergency room. Frank accompanied me while sitting in the room together in pain. I told Frank if the doctor asked me what happened I'm going to tell them that we had a fight he never said a word. sprofoundly he was love more than life, The mystery man came back and pick me up drive me home on our way i told him about the passing of my baby he never show no form of remorse or care he drop me back it was approximately 1.15pm i try to hold his hands to stop him from walking out the door he said Emma i has to go back to work I have to reach Struart by 2.30pm to get Eric he resisted me and leave feel empty all by myself again i started to have on and off cramps and pains like am giving birth naturally. O jesus I continue hiding

Emma

it from najee once she get6 home from school at 4.25pm until then this man never call to check up on me this is so clear that he dont care pains pains, riddling my body leaving wondering and pandering what to do its after 7pm now the blood running down my legs like water pouring out of a broken pipe Frank is now at his second he work for a very large franchised one which i cant disclosed after he where he drop off Fed that where he will be until 11pm. Around 8.10pm I called one of my neighbor upstairs and she come I told her that I lost the baby and I am most go back to the ER cuz I'm in so many pain and losing a lot of blood she said what with Expression A Rose from her face she said Miss Emma you know that I don't drive I can help to take you back to the ER same time my supervisor from Watercrest called me to check up on me she asked how are you doing I explained my circumstances at the present situation and she said give me your address I will come and pick you up which she did we arrived at Darwin square at 9:20 p.m. najee was with us I was rushing by a porter then a nurse said you were here this morning I said yes but I am bleeding so much and in severe pain and I can't stand it they said that they told me to follow up with the OBYGE. I reply Ha said Miss I know but I did not los t my child like this me and frank had an fight that why i have the miscarriage this morning The nurse did not delay she told me that she was calling the police because this is a case between the France on the State of Florida it is domestic dispute and they have to deal with it the way that the law could be too damn to do so a matter of fact I was in fear because I didn't want this to go the wrong way but I could not protect him because I knew this was wrong for him to let me lose the child anyways based on what happened it took me more than an hour to write my statement I was questioned about where me and my daughter would be leaving they told me that says paste and other entity that deal with domestic violence could help us God know I did know where the energy come from I start the right like crazy then the officer took the photograph of my lowest body time it I take a deep breath I had was to free myself from mental slavery and abusive life I want to set an example for my daughter and another woman to let her know that love is nothing like them know that thisc is madness when she got a family she will not live like or life like this I'm sorry an hour as many people I applied myself I came out of the closet I told the truth and not the truth why they're in the ER front start home and noticed that I am not there I told him to come for me at the same place on Darwin Square the police was there waiting for him to be arrested I was still in fear and shaking her asking myself is this the right thing that I'm doing the Lord my chest and head was beating like rain on the roof when you your boom boom boom boom boom boom boom bullet that's how I was shaking and shivering they called him and said why are you still inside I said I get gave me a few minutes he was arrested and charged that morning by the Port Saint Lucie Police for battery and application to a pregnant woman we were taken home by a female officer we run upstairs and straight inside the apartment I was unable to sleep wondering what will be my face in the United the death of America still waiting on my Asylum interview date nothing from immigration I am here still undocument with all of this is going on Lord have mercy God You Are My Strength you're my refuge and my Fortress my help in present time of trouble I continue to pray to the Lord, I pray for strength and peace, I pray for comfort, and reassurance only God knows what I've been going through for the time that I was with the evil man that take me from Miss Fran place to live with him has a house helper, he was very terrible he has cunning has a fox, this man was very cruel, unkind, dreadful as snake mean like star apples I'm doing this because I have the right to set an example for Other Woman and daughters especially those whom has being battered and abused I could not help myself more than to expose him. The truth was what set my soul free. I was free indeed I was blinded by love, over shadow by witch crafts, he was the earth devil or yes sure he was. i learn that infatuation isn't love and spirit take is worse than obeah a good body mean nothing i was punish for his past life he said that he will never love another woman like the way he had love his ex wife whom he brought from Haiti to of American and she leave so in this man heart is empty broken and never counseling he was full of hatred for woman not even prayers could have change him he was lost.

Chapter 13

HIGH HEEL

High Heel, silk dress, natural hair, bright smile name brand clothes, tennis shoes, loafer, matching accessory Lord have mercy I'm Shining like a diamond in the sky purple lipstick that fits my sexy pair of lips that are not cracked and dry like some persons that I knew this on a daily basis two -piece blue and black swimwear, Maxi dress, cut off foot jean, real Jamaican style big earrings hanging on my shoulders glittering low hip jeans i now be a supermodel changing from old Emma to a fashionista pop style. Hot chick i am my own designer, makeup artist too have a nice hair salon in my bathroom i don't have any degree or certificate in this field but i was born gifted now am my own boss enjoying me own company with no one to asked me where am going or am begging a ride not anymore gaining my independence teaches me to value me it was Friday my evening out am heading to Jensen Beach to enjoy dinner by the water Jan's Restaurant A local American Cuisine vegetarian friendly located at 1990 Northeast Jensen Beach Boulevard Florida 34957. This was for girls only two weeks ago one of my co-workers planted couldn't wait for me to

Emma

have some fun reluctantly I got my day off so I was excited. Jennifer call before she drive out of row home she was my knight and Shining Armor and I love her dearly she got there a little bit late Oh my God I asked her if she cannot drive any faster she responded, we're in a 40 speed zone limit typing her fingers on her dashboard we bump into a few stop light on I will we luckily she is a careful driver never disobey the road code I was a little bit 2 HD but we got there just in time before the waiter walks over to our table he said hello and beat us with a warm smile Denise and Jamaica was already seated we introduce each other to the man waiting patiently beside the lovely dining table we sit down killing herself with laughter it was very quiet all I could notice is the fork talking with the plate and the person softly Whispering a little chattering here and there no disturbances the menu book was placed on our table while doing this the guy begun italicize name hey ladies welcome to John's restaurant my name is Bobby toggle add I was looking affect him because I am on the 5 ft 3 in tall I was very short Eden to us when you decided on what you appetizer is please let me grab some broth for you before he left he poured water into a glasses from a clear white water pitcher with in 2 minutes brought was serve I did not undermine the effort nest of the waiter serviced I said to Jamilah I don't even know what to choose Jennifer said l I haven't had beef in a long time She ordered beef barbecue stir fry Johnny said Emma what are you having I said fruit and almond I am watching my weight there they like the delightful guy came back to our order we tried to talk about work being away from when with your unit was awesome I said Relax I couldn't help but to observe the setting of the restaurant I whisper to Johnny's it's beautiful I love the Ambien this was great jameliah our curiosity killing herself we we oh we all make eye contact and everyone laughs at each other the music was off but very calm for me I never enjoy your time like this since I am in the USA I call it Mary marker I wore an all white Romper flew over with a zipper in the middle a Florida cruising the outfit was the most vibrant color that I have seen she was wearing a silver pencil foot jeans suck to her body hey shoes a flat black shoes neatly fitted her Janice here Liu cut with being white frilly Edge a silver Sanders lips lipstick was bright blue glittering from the light above someone has accidentally spilled something on the ground I was so frightened I said whoops the main course taste delicious we all enjoy our meal we talked about covid-19 and how we have to test every 14 days now what work knowing that we were all negative we take off face mask along with us to continue to stay safe we all got we got all kinds of little jokes Jennifer thought it would be interesting for us to order a dark chocolate ganache for this dessert which we all are good to have jameela with whistle the attractive waiters over the the buffet table and went to get our order Johnny said can you imagine that the testing with continent Emma I said Frankly Speaking I don't know when this will ended Jennifer said it's freaking me out at times covid-19 really change our real place intensively it was crazy now I stared at Johnny's as she was lost it her phone out of the conversation fully the waiter come back with this lovely cake well decorated the chocolate dripping on the side raspberry lying on top Jennifer said let's dive in right right away Jonas jump or we all start laughing it was 8:15 p.m. we were ready to leave I think the girl for a wonderful

Emma

night jameela leave a $10 tip for the waiter the even with still keep our distance while we exit the building we bid goodbye to each other and drive out one behind the other two have to work on Saturday me and Janice I was tired I didn't say much to Jennifer we stop by my neighbor house pick up now and headed over to my place and nice grey and white apartment she drop us off and I just said Auntie Jennifer goodnight I love you Jennifer see love you too I said see you soon and thanks again I went inside for najee right away to bed I took a cold shower and slept it was Saturday a new feelings I was fresh feeling perfect I have to take Lyft to work it take a quick wash get waited 7 minutes for my taxi to arrive at work it was one of my residents now become an incompetent patient I had to change her twice doing break fast she looked nervous stop in the face business I reassured her that it's fine and she wasn't a problem I am only doing my best and I love you dearly but I couldn't help smiling when she said I am old old God everyday is an extra-ordinary one especially at memory care unit I comforted her and ask her what can I do to let her feel better she said a cup of coffee I said find after I get your dress and back in the dining room you get your coffee I said ever heard of scrambled egg sweet rolls table butter plenty of hot coffee after everyone has their breakfast weekly in the area and place them in the TV room my day went fast I did my 8 hours and clocked out I get home and make some pumpkin soup for me and Najee France add feet away for good last in the outer blue no word about him since he left for Miami in April life is much better now I am stable so it was not Nightfall not to wash the dishes take a shower brush your teeth then we watch the Jamaican news I become overwhelmed with the thought about the man that I had loved and trusted and thought he understand me we are now separated I come to realize right there sitting on the toilet bowl letting letting go isn't simple but for me it was done it was over after months of not seeing him I allow my mind not to blunder Noddy shop mommy are you okay I was not part of my thought yes I'm fine and I will be out soon sometime unexpected the other happen it was for the best 1 week after my coworker drop me home around 11:47 p.m. I got home I went straight to bed I was exhausted I jump into bed with my uniform on I did I did was to take my shoes off laying down when I noticed my phone light up well I said to myself who could this be now to my surprise friends we send me a friend request on Facebook I was surprised friend sent me and my friend request isn't this strange knowing that he's still on probation why would he do such a thing curiosity drives me wild I question myself what is this that motivate him now I was scared as hell I could not fell asleep I twist I tossed I turned and roll from left to right is this clash of the Titan or Avatar I Prayed Again to God's suddenly for the I need to breathe some fresh air in. I become fatigued and inconsolable sad memory of this man haunting me that I think twice I get out of my bedroom finally, I drink a glass of water swallow hard this must be a nightmare or night demons I turned off my phone and do my breathing techniques on my back until I fell asleep. Their was one imagination keep on coming back to me about Frank it was captivating the reality of who he was and what's so special about him I quickly the blotted him out my mind it over actually I am Having Goosebumps all over my skin the lost lingering my mind I am left without an answer questions no

Emma

apology I was terrified Sunday I was up early I called Mom and Dad and the rest of children back home in Jamaica does the insurer that they're taking their medication at Eating on time it was drought hot humid and clammy my mom told me that there was no water in the pipe is having rain 4 months now I put my old gospel on make pancake scramble egg with cheese with some fresh fruit serve with cottage cheese I have my devotion with God for 30 minutes after I take my shower I drink a lot of water because I was dreaming already by my lost and I have been progressing well by picking up the pieces and trodding on by faith extremely happy I stared to spend lot more time at work getting recognition and brainstorming gathering the fact and moving forward time fly a get my first new old car from one of my coworker a 2019 Chevy Malibu gold I never have a driver license, oniy a learner license therefore I wouldnt drive certain time by myself Kathy call me 3 days in advance to come and collect the the honest truth is that i was afraid of driving in the usa anyway i went for my car License and insured taking my own time until i understand the road code one night i got pull over by the cops for running a red but i gotten a warning thank goddess It's the first time that I ever drove this fast I got home take a shower to bed there was truly a time in life when I think I would not elevate myself but this is my turning point now that Nagi got a scholarship attending a private school straight on the principal honor is only jah jah blessing thing just happening one year past it christmas i bake our favorite jamaican fruit cake fry chicken, gungo rice and peas, real old sorrel drink, white overproof white rum some rum punch curry goat and mannish water jerk chicken, hot and spicy gather a few friends that i have met in the nursing field we enjoy the afternoon listening to some cultural reggae music eating and drinking our caribbean food the news of covid 19 been to raised so we came under lock down one of the harder time for me working 24 hours everyone become anti social dealing with this weird pandemic vurtiual learning was the most ideal setting for my daughter to attend school a lot of callous remark about the decision hurt some parents feeling but they were no other better choice than to keep the children home for their own health safety because everyone was at risk to catch this deadly disease I work long hours using a ecam to monitor my child from home precaution measure were implement throught over facility x shortage of ppe gears have us washing mask every week even some of my coworkers quit i would be at work for 3 days and 3 nights due nurse and assistant nurses calling out lord have mercy this was normal lot of family members get upset rathering, confused fail to understand why, why, months run of we lost so many patient to mr covid sudden die is like a death demons sweeping the land every establish was closed no toilet paper or drinking water the city is miserable but thank god me and najee wasnt apart of the rush at home plenty toilet paper, cases of water, canned food, cereals, and canned vegetables is was chaos children becoming depressed not been able to handle the shut but my bible told me that perilous time shall come unemployment step in homes in problems broken home lost of their love no babysitter was allowed to work parents had to give up the job file for government benefits small business owner losing thousand of dollars daily has caregiver we work under lots of pressure scary moment everything crumble i feel the pains of the

Emma

family within a week the memory care unit lost 8 patients Because I want to go fast with this looking after the third patient we were more scared about our own safety people did not understand what is going on the inside there are days when we could not perform our regular task life as change vividly no one could understand this unknown covid virus but we work assiduously doing what we can just to save life because that was our duty no matter first responder september 23 i resigned my job at Watercrest Funny enough I apply to the Ark of st. Lucie by the time I settle down in this new city Fort Pierce I was ready to revamped and enjoy this beautiful community this city carry so much attraction an adventure great building manatees beautiful see line and chords to Shore and wonderful coral reefs every Sunday you see people surfing on the beach it was exciting you I used to go out on the boat to start sightseeing and enjoy the beautiful ocean that there especially the jetty it's his one wonderful attraction that I would not forget I always took the children there to enjoy a wonderful especially on of my day off Najee loves the water The seagull, the Falcon the peacock there was some special birds in this area they walk across the street without fear any you have to be careful not to hit I enjoy eating at the carby from upstairs is a elegant scenery Watching the high wave rocking the boats always Dine In Style no disturbances very quiet lovely ambience most of all very intriguing Everyone was so grateful to be out after almost two years in lockdown the governor decide that it's about time we continue living or life even though they covid-19 wasn't so high but there were still precautionary measure that we got to take you can lay on I'm the beautiful beach and watch the sunset it was so beautiful it seems like we're just noticing life everything try to return to normal but we still got to live our life on a daily basis just to ensure that we can have an open mind and continue living downtown was congestive they have a festival and everybody wanted to be there music playing people dancing there was also a gospel concert we went to enjoy the afternoon we were well dressed in our best dressed and meeting friends and family for a long time back home I told my mom and dad to take all the necessary care of themselves because of their health condition my granddaughter was diagnosed with covid-19 I was so scared for her because she already have sickle cell he prayed and we prayed and we prayed and she pulled through with school closing down they have to study at home also in Jamaica suddenly I got a call that my aunt and my pastor was diagnosed my pastor died my aunt linger for a little bit but months after she was deceased also the family was in mourning because Auntie was the best person we have to guide us she was a lifesaver she was the one that instill everything in us and motivate us to be who we are she supported me coming to America and I'm wondering who's going to take care of Nixon and Brooke I know that the kids were at University but I'm wondering if any one of them is going to come back to be in the house she have a beautiful home with a lovely back yard very spacious and a great Garden we didn't have to ask for anything she provide everything the family needed I was saddened to know that covid 19 rob me I usually say that I am praying that none of my family would go through this ordeal and this monster to take any of them I was last 4 Words once more in a desolate that situation I could not explain how this pain is going to go her way knowing that she was the only person we could ever turn to end our life when we have family situation you would always pray with us and through US eventually she was very within 3 weeks I send some money home to help with the funeral procession but I asked God to keep us together make us one bind us together and give us any peace and give us confident to continue living my siblings went on to London all three of them are there with the rest of the family so my son remained with my mom and one of my sister Tamika still there she's now a teacher at the prominent High School in Jamaica he had to work from home iI break the news to Movetta and her children she was my only cousin here She lives in Port Saint Lucie everybody has the morn separately we could not get together because we were cautioned to stay away all we could do is call and talk to each other the console one another a great big lost a super great lost but we are urging each other to stay strong and United 1 back to reality I did a full year at Arc of Saint Lucie by this time I was diagnosed with the covid virus myself I got no symptoms no headache, no sign nothing I was quarantine for 21 days When they tested my daughter she was negative so we were speculating how could I be positive but at that time there was some fake positive going around so I was sent back to work immediately sitting at home it was boring Couldn't wait to go back to work a new job a new environment I apply to work at Longwood Hospital as a housekeeper during my tenant here at the previous things start falling apart No supervisor, management getting fired it was just so unbelievable how this entity is losing their value so I decide to move on with great expectation I went in and I did a wonderful job within four months on the job I was awarded one of the most exceptional worker at Lawnwood Regional Hospital I decided to rise above the level I asked my director if I can move into a different position I didn't apply to work as a Patient Care Techincian at the new tower that was going to open in June of this year 2022. I got the position when the training apply to the situation and move on because I believe that I can rise above any situation being in this department is a new settings for me but I open my mind, my brain my heart my gathering the facts that will help me to perform my duty not familiarize with a lot of the new equipment because at Watercrest and the Arc of St. Lucie we didn't have these high-tech machines. My first month wasn't easy it was a test run but I pulled through with the help of my new coworkers everyone was a team we work together we never criticize each other or be little each other because we are always there our job and to offer the best care to these patients they here to provide all the love and comfort in helping them to recuperate this is lawnwood team above all else we are commit care and improve of human life. on my days off I would strolled to the botanical garden it was one of the most relaxing moment for me to see Birds attractive waterfalls beautiful spring with you huge freshwater fish, octopus, jellyfish People moving up and down eating and drinking as they indulge in their own activity we were surrounded by water flower huge tree The birds sounds so sweet chittering in the trees above Clear Blue Skies Ahead right and sunny day was what's a wonderful scenery I realized that I have one of the greatest experience ever I am enjoying my life this memory will be Unforgettable I hear the Roar of the Wind as we approach another area of the garden Lot of wildlife in the inhabitants huge iguana lizards running up and

Emma

down lovely green complexion the sun light exposing this rich bright color on them they are beautiful species naturally colorful. No one seems to be excited more than I do because it means so much to me to get a day off from the Hospital Reluctantly for me I so slowly across the wooden bridge that join that other area of the garden from where I was standing the water rushing down the slope leading into the wide ocean isn't that amazing then I left for the library where I exchange my book and my daughter with change hers also, we enjoy reading Novels because we specialized in Romance and mystery drama and detective story i find them very exciting reading is fun for me because I always wanted to be a detective or a police officer. Has I grew up I realized that my career part change I become one of the best caregiver that the world I've ever known when am away from work is a magical moment for me I felt like a fairy standing in that garden surrounded by butterflies can you imagine the sunset looking at it from a distant over hill observing it seems that like the entire city has been light up, such a beautiful Radiance that's sparks shining so bright with it orange color it was a marvelous sight then came a sudden shower of rain we run into the car and sit their for a watching the dark cloud covering the beauty lighting flashing the thunder start roll the evening change so we set off an headed for the weather change completely all gray sky running rushing on the streets it became foggy i high my wiper and drive slowly on US Highway we were 10 minutes from home has soon as we approach the driveway the rain was slightly falling it was heavy anymore we couldn't exit the vehicle no raincoat, no umbrella i never mine having one or the other because I always forgot them somewhere the outside light come on automatically so you know that is dark now we have no choice more than to run upstairs in the rain that remind me when i was a child growing up jamaica it usually rains in May and Otober and during the hurricanes season in those days we had to take our shoes off wrap up our books in plastic bags some of us shelter under the green banana leave or the cocoa leave other used newspaper to make hats at time we would be soaking wet by the time get home our parents will be boiling tea for us to keep us warm and make sure our head dry properly to prevent cold the rain who beat on the roof like bullets and when the lighting flash we hide under the sheet especially if it night time lord have mercy we fall asleep quick quick boil dumpling, boil banana and curry chicken or pepper pot soup and cornmeal porridge u lick you finger food so sweet who sleep angel feed them that what mother said ah me never sleep so those were my great day i enjoy those day then it was good i went right into the kitchen make some tea and eat some left over foods and headed straight to bed i am comfortable now doing me was the greatest thing that i learn to value over the years life teach me to love first me to all the person who fell like their life can change and your only intention is to give up stay strong keeping praying stop thinking suicide get family support i encourage you to ride out the storm i am a survivor a powerful women of faith and thats why i am alive to today i want you to know that you can make it too dont be an alcoholic, or a drug addict it only make the situation instead a friend when you need a friend life is not what you make i believe it what happen morally dont not sit in the seat of discornful walk proud hold your head up height go for whatever you needed jesus

Emma

in your life you dont have to go to church the church is inside of you prayers is the greatest weapon to fight your battles venegance is mines said the lord he fight mines for me and today am happy women and rejoicing i make it no one is above the law god will give you desering eye your fly high challenge we must face hurdles we must crossed and bridges we must burned love is kind and patient my peace i leave with you dont not be afraid for iam with you said the of host angel in heaven are protecting each and everyone of us this story is areal life story base on Emma journey.

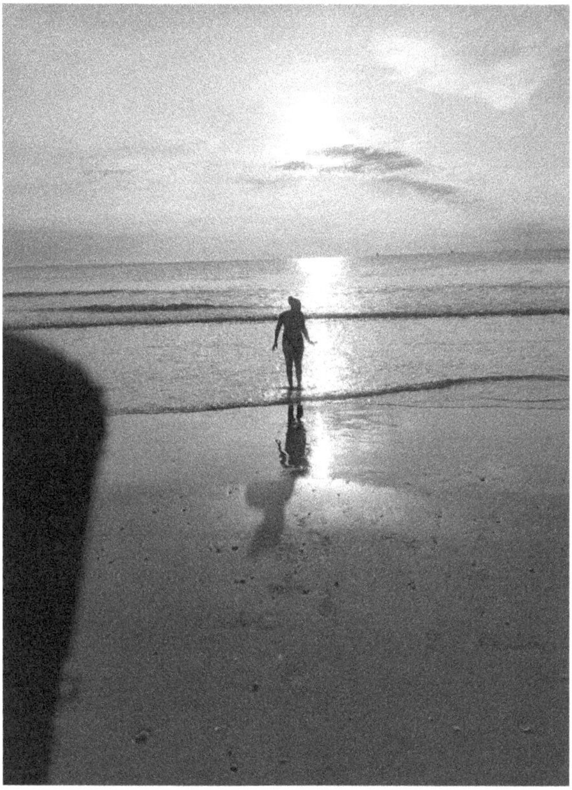

Chapter 14

THE CITY

I move over to a new city rejoicing and lifting the name of Jesus. There are no mountains that you can't climb, no chains that can't be broken. My supervisors, managers, coworkers were my team and everyone was my main supporters. I was glad I met a lot of great women and men on this journey called life. I was optimistic and Infused for all the love and support that she shows to me. To my avocate from Safe Space for Domestic Violence who have provide me with relocations funds to help me pay my rent, food, clothing for me and my daughter lord i thank you for your grace to everyone out their that going to read my book that think your situation is bad alot of us have a story some of which break us, build us, and mold us just remember that people do change, things change life in general change but hold on to jesus because faith is the substance of all things living in style owning my own car graining education working in a safe environment i am breathing newness of life since i move out of the apartment i change my mailing address i only set my eyes on the evil man three times my fake wedding dress is still in the wrapper the exact

Emma

way it came from Amazon and the rings end up somewhere that i don't even remember my life is better than before I heard that the move to Miami and leave his best friends live in the apartment by their reported but take care until we meet again in glory land and stay safe and remember to pray for the Forgiveness of your sins I am here to tell someone that your master is waiting to raise you up no matter what obstacle faced you in life just believe in the word of the Lord I must close this chapter of my life so many baturin struggles and difficult to teach me not to give up because life is worth living and my children my siblings my parents and other family membersthey give me the Zeal to continue to reach out for this sky I'm a proud mom will stand up against domestic violence and against woman that believe there is no help I know it's hard to let the agony, pain, trauma, nightmare and fear go but put God first in your life. I stand in accordance with each and everyone of you throughout the world we are survivors if i make it you too can make it to these hard working persons I appreciate you all with sincere gratitude to my loved one god bless your heart for this too shall pass, we are like star lights that sparkle in the sky I am a winner and winners never quit, pressed on with faith God promises never to leave us nor forsake us. I went on to become a great achiever. I obtained my High school diploma, a certificate in certified Nursing Assistant, Diploma Child Development Association certificate Registered Behavioural Technician from Autism Partnership Foundation Home Health Aide certified. I now enroll at Ashworth College doing a four year degree Paralegal with a lot more behind my name. My smiles and laughter are now my joy along with 6 children and seven grandchildren. I can say that I am truly blessed. Thank you all for your love and support Najee and I love you always. I will continue to stand up and support woman in need of help throughout the world, who are battered and scared and do not know which road to take I will endorsed everyone to stand tall and be not afraid of anything and open up, help is there safespace the churches and other entity will provide the necessary help you require and to law enforcement team thank you for your job a well done a special thank you to the amazing team at State Attorney I thank you to my lawyer and Healing water counseling teams names I cant disclosed thanks for your support I endorse your effort I have a great and spontaneous Journey with, as we continue to pray to God for his mercy endureth forever and ever more amen.

Chapter 15

THE CLOSURER

My life wasn't the best we weren't hungry after Frank was arrested God send so many different persons in my life, I've always depend on him to take me everywhere God move him out of my life for me to prosper and grow all these events took place after the disaster in my word 'it was cold Thursday morning. I was standing right in front of the apartment at Leacock Run. I was on my way to work still feeling hopeless, I know that I have no choice more than to walk to work if I didn't get a ride I was literally bumping ride that particular day My legs was weary, shaky and tired I walked back and forth to work every single day since Fratz was in jail, now that he was out on bond he was order to stay away from us the fact that the death of our child has shattered everything that i hope and prayer was taken my mind started to feel guilty unrested negative thought displaying but i brace myself and focus on the future ahead of me my mine switched like a light bulk i heard a voice saying to sing this song am not my own i belong to jesus it was 6.20am while i was walking i see a bright light coming i stress out my hands and flogged the vehicle down it stop i said good

Emma

morning mom can you please give a ride to California Boulevard the lady did not hesitated she said sure, i hopped in the car it was a beautiful spanish lady heading to work herself she was going to stuart she told me that we can exchange numbers and promise me that she can drop me to work during the week only because she doesnt work on the weekend she asked me if i drive i told her no am i am in a tight situation at the moment i have been walking to work in the cold, the rain and the sun she told me her name and exchange our numbers we arrived at my destination within 10 minutes o boy felt so realized i was very grateful i said for your kind gratitude i give god thank for his blessing she now become my best friend she drove me to work for a whole month and never asked for a penny. one morning i told her my misfortune and the lost of my child that causes me to be struggling on my own she then explained to me that she herself has a similar story and that i am not alone she was also abuse an a victim of domestic violence, she encourage me and told me t6hat i must worry you did the right by getting the man arrested she said that his family will always choose him over you no matter what, stand up for your right and do not fear for god to get everything under control. she also promised me if i didn't get anywhere to live with me and my daughter can stay by her house. I started to hold myself together knowing that there is no shame in what I did night I would give praise he's constantly unto the Lord asking him to find me a place to live I was given an offer by safe space to come by Elton Stewart if we couldn't find a place I went on Facebook and I got up late when I went to the lady told me that it is only for one person but i got my daughter she said I don't care it's only for one person.

I left feeling miserable and angry and my heart was crying. He was my life she has a great future ahead of her we went back to leacock Run feeling like a drink I cuddle up on the sofa with tears rolling down my face swapping hard my mind flashed back on made in Frank but deep inside I knew that I would have to get up shake up myself wipe my face and hit social media I was searching through listing and classify a statement about cheap place that is there renting I eventually saw one post and hour ago oh my God I call the person so fast the guy answer I am at work but meet me at 5 p.m. and I'm going to send you my details I said okay thank you and see you soon I got a ride drove to where he promised to meet each other at the time I got $1,860 in cash on me he was a Spanish guy around 5 feet 1 inch tall low-cut here seem pretty young invite me Najee and the other person inside his apartment he told me his name I didn't introduce myself also I was giving a tour it was a beautiful bedroom painted it white bathroom was too so spacious I said to him fine I will take it he throw the key to my daughter and said see you on Friday I pay my deposit and said see you on Friday on Spotify get my receipt and redo parted I give God thanks again because Merica continue to generate in my life by the time I arrived at these cut wrong I call my house will get done told her the good news she told me that on Friday we must meet at the thrift shop called Safe on US1 in Port st. Lucie West I told the judge inside the courthouse that when I'm leaving I would not take any of this mysterious person possession from the premises because they belongs to him and that place is comfort his zone I got a driver on Thursday request that I hired a U-Haul for an hour to move me out of the turmoil, depression and sad

Emma

place where I was so unrest, ah yes it's Friday am I was leaving me and Najee was up pretty early so we started to pack the truck up, with all of our stuff and belongings the only thing I take was a bed that Frank gave to Najee amazingly grateful I couldn't wait to sleep in a new environment, God has blessed me with everything that I pray for I host needed to be called a home of all necessities we dragged behind us over suitcase I was glowing like a new rose bursting out of it petal I know that it is my turning point, in my life and new beginning, new era told days are gone and wash away mystery, adventurous and magical dimension await us. We unpack all of our clothes in less than an hour, my smile came back, my blood pressure went on the control I felt like a new creature on this earth, I was Flying Without Wings, no longer chuckled by fear, or bandage of the flesh. I put my foot in paul shoes when he got blind on his way to Damascus I love the book of romans colossians and psalms they were truly was an inspiration in my everyday endeavor reading the bible motivate me And going to counseling once more at Healing Waters there was an illustration that taught me how to feel around other I never believe in failure I rise up like an eagle sowing to new high because has Bob Marley said emancipate yourself from mental salvary none but ourselves can free our minds so i let go off the pains, hurt and free myself i listen to my voice that become the voice of a praying mother brave full of coverage and i encourage all battered, abuse, woman who left to face humiliation and discrimination to join a place that will help you survived the long suffering you are strong be a role model for the women of tomorrows society only u can stop the crime fight with all your might god is our strength.

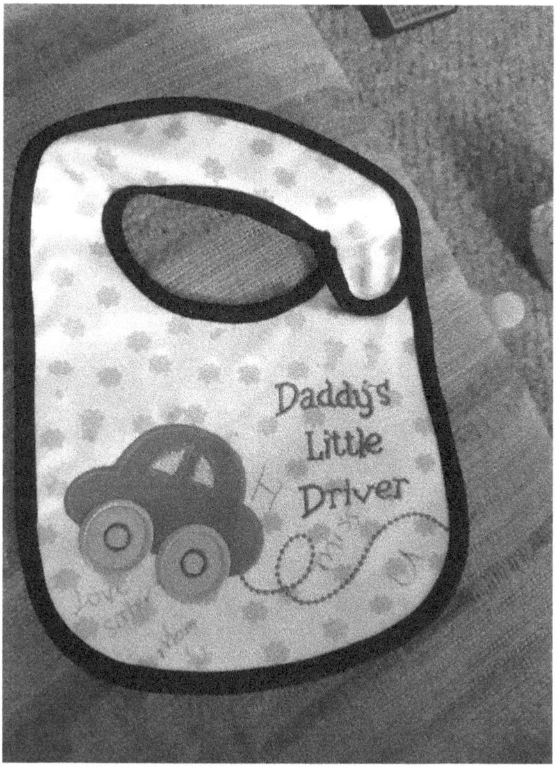
Daddy's
Little
Driver

CPSIA information can be obtained
at www.ICGtesting.com
Printed in the USA
BVHW040355160323
660405BV00015BA/970/J

9 781665 579544